I0489966

CEO Guide to Doing Business in Japan

By Ade Asefeso MCIPS MBA

Second Edition

ISBN-13: 978-1499543124

ISBN-10: 1499543123

Publisher: AA Global Sourcing Ltd
Website: http://www.aaglobalsourcing.com

Table of Contents

Disclaimer

This publication is designed to provide competent and reliable information regarding the subject matter covered. However, it is sold with the understanding that the author and publisher are not engaged in rendering professional advice. The authors and publishers specifically disclaim any liability that is incurred from the use or application of contents of this book.

If you purchased this book without a cover you should be aware that this book may have been stolen property and reported as "unsold and destroyed" to the publisher. In this case neither the author nor the publisher has received any payment for this "stripped book."

Dedication

This book is dedicated to the hundreds of thousands of incredible souls in the world who have weathered through the up and down of recent recession.

To my family and friends who seems to have been sent here to teach me something about who I am supposed to be. They have nurtured me, challenged me, and even opposed me.... But at every juncture has taught me!

This book is dedicated to my lovely boys, Thomas, Michael and Karl. Teaching them to manage their finance will give them the lives they deserve. They have taught me more about life, presence, and energy management than anything I have done in my life.

Introduction

Are you a CEO, consultant or entrepreneur interested in entering or expanding your activity in the Japanese market?

Then this guide is for you!

The main objective of CEO guide to doing business in Japan is to provide you with basic knowledge about Japan; an overview of its economy, business culture, potential opportunities and an introduction to other relevant issues. Novice exporters, in particular will find this book a useful starting point.

Japan is one of the world's largest economies. In 2009 Japan's economy (in US Dollar terms and using current prices) was 4 times the size of India, 3 times the size of South Korea and 2 times the size of the UK.

Japan is the UK's largest export market after Europe and the US, and Britain was Japan's tenth largest market in 2009. Total export of goods and services from UK to Japan in 2009 stood at £8.1bn.

Britain and Japan are key strategic partners. There are approximately 17,000 British citizens residing in Japan and approximately 52,000 Japanese living in the UK.

You need a long-term commitment and market strategy to set up in Japan. It takes time and patience, but as many British companies have found, it can repay the effort many times over.

Strengths of the market; in brief these are:
- Open economy.
- Cutting edge technology and R&D. Japan has 2% of the world's population but 20% of global R&D spend with an emphasis on technologies to deliver a low carbon future and to support the ageing population. There were 390,000 patent applications received in 2008 and 177,000 patents issued.
- Japan's 127m consumers are highly educated, demand the highest standards and are early adopters.
- Japan is a strategic stepping stone for other Asian markets.

Opportunities in Japan

There are more than 400 British companies enjoying success in Japan including visible high street names such as Lush, Top Shop and Burberry as well as HSBC, GlaxoSmithKline and Rolls-Royce.

The UK's services industry is also very active, from design to legal, financial and consultancy services.

Key sectors where there are opportunities for UK exports of goods and services:
- Aerospace
- Automotive
- Bio/pharma

- Chemicals
- Computer software and games
- Creative industries (fashion, design, music)
- Energy
- Fashion
- Financial and legal services
- Food and drink
- Healthcare
- Telecommunications

The ageing population is expected to result in the creation of new goods and services targeting seniors.

Chapter 1: Economic and Political Overview

In 2009 exports from the UK to Japan were £8.1 billion. Imports from Japan to the UK were £9.9 billion. Exports in 2012 so far are dominated by four major sectors:

- Healthcare
- Machinery
- Chemicals and
- Transport equipment.

Japan is one of the world's largest exporters and one of the largest overseas investors. Economic growth is heavily export dependent, despite exports only accounting for around 13% of GDP in 2009 (in the UK exports accounted for around 27% of GDP). At 3.9% of GDP, foreign direct investment into Japan is low but the Japanese government is aiming to increase this.

Small and medium sized enterprises make up 99.5% of all Japanese companies. The service sector accounts for 67% of total gross value added with manufacturing accounting for 22%.

Key challenges for the Japanese economy after 20 years of low growth are how to raise growth, reverse price deflation, deal with a high and rising public sector debt and adapt to a rapidly ageing society.

The current population of Japan is around 127 million people. A declining birth rate and high longevity mean a rapidly ageing population, with 20% already 65 or over. This is predicted to rise to 40% by 2050, by when the population is predicted to have fallen to 95 million. Most Japanese live in densely populated urban areas. The Tokyo conurbation remains the world's largest at around 35m.

Like the UK, Japan has a monarchy, with a parliamentary government split between an Upper and Lower House. Emperor Akihito is the current Head of State.

After over 50 years of almost continuous rule by the Liberal Democratic Party (LDP), a General Election in August 2009 saw a landslide victory for the opposition Democratic Party of Japan, led by Yukio Hatoyama. The manifesto policies that helped bring the DPJ into power focused on social welfare, with a pledge to raise the necessary funds by eliminating waste and cutting unnecessary projects. The DPJ also wants to change the internal workings of Government, reducing the influence of civil servants and the traditionally close government links to big business.

Hatoyama resigned in June 2010 and was replaced by Naoto Kan who had been Finance Minister.

Chapter 2: Getting there and Advice About your Stay

There are daily direct international flights from Heathrow to Tokyo. The international airport for Tokyo (Narita) is 1 hour by train from central Tokyo. Western Japan is served by Kansai International Airport, with flights from eg Frankfurt, Paris and Amsterdam, but no direct UK flights.

Getting around

Public transport is safe, reliable, easy to use and fast. Do not take a taxi from the airport to downtown Tokyo unless you are prepared for a long ride and a huge bill.

Visas

UK citizens are able to enter Japan for a period of 6 months or less without needing a visa. For further advice we advise you to check the website of the Embassy of Japan in the UK (http://www.uk.emb-japan.go.jp/en).

Your stay

Japan is still mainly a cash-based society. You should always ensure that you have enough cash with you. Credit cards are accepted at major hotels, shops, high-class restaurants and in some taxis, though UK cards do not always work. Many smaller shops, restaurant and train stations will not take credit cards.

Addresses can be hard to find and tend not to use street names. It's always a good idea to have a map (preferably in Japanese if you are taking a taxi) for the location of meetings, restaurants etc. Allow ample time to get there.

British companies wishing to approach the Japanese market are advised to undertake as much market research and planning as possible.

In most cases, exporting to Japan requires working through local business partners, such as an agent or distributor.

This will only be a first step. Personal relationships are very important in this market and should be developed with a long-term perspective, built on mutual trust. This requires patience, an investment of time and personal presence. Regular visits to the market are an important part of a successful interaction with the agent/distributor.

Chapter 3: What to Consider when Doing Business in Japan

Above all, be patient. Do not expect quick returns. They may come. But for many Japanese companies, the emphasis is more on developing the sort of trust and mutual confidence that will lead to a strong, enduring relationship than on getting down to business instantly. This is why Japan is a market requiring a strategic approach rather than an opportunistic one. It is also why the potential for long-term achievement is so great.

When developing a relationship with a potential Japanese partner:

- Expect questions and follow-up quickly on any requests for information. It may not seem so important to you but the Japanese side may be very keen on details.
- Develop and maintain relationships.
- Make regular visits to the market.
- Treat "test orders" very seriously.
- Remember that after sales service is very important.

Key areas for business

Although the greater Tokyo metropolitan area and Osaka are the two largest commercial areas, there are regional clusters and opportunities; depending on the sector. The Japan External Trade Organization

15

(JETRO) provides in-depth profiles of Japan's regions at http://www.jetro.go.jp/en/invest/region).

Market entry and start up Considerations

JETRO produce a guide to "Laws & Regulations on Setting Up Business in Japan" here http://www.jetro.go.jp/en/invest/setting_up/laws/.

Customs and Regulations

The Japan Customs website is a useful source of information. Their website is at http://www.customs.go.jp/english.

Legislation and Local Regulations

Companies are best advised to seek legal/taxation advice before entering into a joint venture or similar type of partnership.

Recruiting and Retaining Staffing

Lifetime employment used to be a dominant feature in Japanese companies but this has been crumbling as companies seek to reduce costs and younger employees are more open to the idea of changing jobs. The recruitment market had been growing steadily until the global financial crisis and international recruitment agencies such as Michael Page, Robert Walters and Manpower have offices in Japan. There is a plethora of recruitment agencies/headhunters who cater for personnel needs of foreign companies ranging from junior support staff to CEO.

Many are members of the British Chamber of Commerce in Japan.

Job mobility is higher in sectors such as finance, IT and consumer goods but less so in the more traditional manufacturing industry. There has been an increase in English speaking job seekers but it can still be difficult to find candidates with English language ability and experience and knowledge of a certain business sector, particularly if the sector is in a technological niche area.

Dismissal of staff is not easy. There is considerable precedent in case law to the effect that it is necessary to meet certain criteria (e.g. selection of affected staff has been made reasonably) in order for the dismissal to be deemed reasonable.

Standards and Technical Regulation

Japanese domestic standards often differ from international norms. The Japanese Standards Association has a website at http://www.jsa.or.jp/default_english.asp

Intellectual Property Rights

Patent, utility model, trademark, copyrights and design are the main intellectual property rights associated with trade and industry and there are

Japanese laws governing the registration and protection of these rights.

Japan's trademark law offers equal protection for Japanese and foreign nationals. UK companies with an intention to develop business in Japan can register their trademarks with Japan Patent

Office (JPO) even if they do not have an office in Japan (NB: provided that the trademarks are used within 3 years after registration). Japan adopts a "first-to-file" principle which means that a trademark can be registered even if it is not yet in use. Once registered, a trademark is protected for 10 years.

The "first-to-file" principle applies also to patents and it is advisable not to publicise an invention until it has been registered. The protection period for patents is 20 years.

Details on the registration procedures and the fees involved can be found in the JPO website (www.jpo.go.jp).

Chapter 4: Business Etiquette, Language and Culture

Casual American-style attire is still uncommon in the Japanese business place. You should dress appropriately for the occasion when meeting your counterparts on business.

When sitting down to a business meeting with your Asian counterparts, the seating arrangement will be determined by the status of the participants. Do not just sit anywhere; as the guest, you will be directed to the appropriate seat.

As a general rule, the highest ranking person from the host side will sit at the head of the table. Then, other people will take their seats starting from the seats closest to him and working to the other end of the table. Those of higher status sit closest to the "head honcho".

You should stand at your seat and wait for the top guy to tell you to be seated. Then, when the meeting is finished, wait until he has stood up before standing up yourself.

Non-alcoholic drinks will probably be served at the beginning of the meeting and they will be distributed in the order of descending importance of recipients. You may want to wait for the top guy to drink from his glass before starting on yours.

Gifts are always appreciated. Consider bringing a small souvenir that represents well your hometown to give to your host. Don't be surprised if your hosts give you something from their country too. If the gift is wrapped, don't open it until you leave. If the gift is not wrapped, make sure to express copious appreciation (whether you like it or not). Ask some questions about the gift to show interest.

You may want to take notes during the meeting. This will show that you are interested and will be appreciated by your hosts. However, you should make certain never to write anyone's name in red ink (even your own) and so carry a black or blue pen.

Japanese is the only official language. Since World War II, all Japanese have studied English at school and English is spoken by growing numbers. But few people other than officials, academics and businessmen who are in frequent contact with foreigners can speak it well.

Bear in mind many Japanese are too polite to let you know when they do not fully understand. Keep what you say simple and straightforward. The same is true if an interpreter is used. Speak in short bursts, which can be easily translated. Don't ask rhetorical questions. Avoid idioms.

Keep any jokes very simple. And don't try to do business in Japanese unless you are very confident indeed. For follow-up meetings at least, you should provide your own interpreter, as a matter of basic courtesy. Please note this can be quite expensive.

The Japanese prefer not to display strong emotion in public. If you show shock or anger during business negotiations, they will believe that you lack self-control and are questionable as a business partner.

The younger members of your team should generally remain quiet and defer to their seniors during the meetings.

The Japanese may ask international visitors many questions, including information about your job, your title, your age, your responsibilities, the number of employees that report to you, etc.

Japanese is a very complex language with many forms of address and honorifics. They will need a lot of information to decide which form to use when speaking to you.

Punctuality, Appointments, and Local Time

- Be punctual at all times. Tardiness is considered rude.
- During three weeks of the year (New Year's holidays, December 28 to January 3; Golden Week, April 29 to May 5; and Obon, in Mid-August), many people visit the graves of their ancestors. Conducting business and travelling are difficult during these periods.
- Japan is nine hours ahead of Greenwich Mean Time, or 14 hours ahead of Eastern Standard Time.

Negotiating

- Be polite and nice, but don't be ingratiating out of fear of offending.

- A positive, persuasive presentation works better with the Japanese than does a high-pressure, confrontational approach.

- Negotiations are occasionally begun at the middle level and continued at the executive level.

- Connections are very helpful in Japan. Do not choose someone of lower rank than the person with whom he or she will be negotiating. Intermediaries should not be part of either company involved in the deal. If you don't have a connection, a personal call is better than a letter or e-mail.

- Use an intermediary to convey bad news.

- Using a Japanese lawyer rather than a Western one indicates a cooperative spirit.

- The Japanese usually use the initial meetings to get to know you, while at the same time asking to hear about your proposal. Agreements of confidentiality are vague.

- Contracts are not perceived as final agreements. You or they may later renegotiate.

- Because age equals rank, show the greatest respect to the oldest members of the Japanese group with whom you are in contact.

- You will not be complimented on good work, because the group and not the individual is rewarded. It is a bad idea to single out Japanese workers.

- Do not make accusations or refuse anything directly; be indirect.

- At work the Japanese are very serious and do not try to "lighten things up" with humour.

- When working with Japanese who know English, or when using an interpreter, be patient. Speak slowly, pause often, and avoid colloquialisms. Your interpreter may seem to be taking more time with the translation than you did with your statement; this is because she or he is using lengthy forms of respect.
- At times, you may need to pretend you are sure that your Japanese colleague or friend has understood you, even if you know this is not the case. This is important for maintaining a good relationship.

A few words of Japanese can go a long way. Here are a few commonly-used phrases: English Japanese
- Good morning (used up to about 10am) Ohayou gozaimasu
- Hello / Good day (used from about 10am) Konnichiwa
- Good evening Konbanwa
- Good night Oyasumi nasai
- Goodbye Sayounara
- Excuse me Sumimasen
- I am sorry Gomen nasai
- Thank you Arigatou
- Yes (I've heard you) Hai
- No Iie

The EU-Japan Centre for Industrial Co-operation (www.eujapan.com) offers language training programmes and study tours

Chapter 5: Meetings and Presentations

Despite what some books say about the uniqueness of Japan, there is nothing mystical about doing business in Japan. Business is business here as elsewhere, and increasingly cosmopolitan. So you need not worry unduly about the niceties of Japanese etiquette. But here our top ten tips:

- Take things slowly. Follow the advice under language above.
- Never be late. Punctuality is crucial! Japanese cities are crowded and can be complicated to get around. Leave plenty of time to allow for traffic hold-ups. Keep to the timetable for your meetings. Don't try to change or cancel appointments at the last minute unless you have absolutely no alternative. Don't overrun the designated period unless your interlocutor clearly wants to extend it.
- Take business cards with you and have plenty available. They should preferably be printed in Japanese on the reverse and be standard size (90 x 55mm). Business cards in other sizes do not fit the card boxes which sit on practically every Japanese desk and so may be discarded.
- Construct a short but warm introductory statement for each meeting. This should not be a sales pitch. It should explain why you are here, how long you will be here, the sort of people you are seeing and any particular previous contact you have had with

Japan. You could refer briefly to the long-standing warm ties between the UK and Japan. If appropriate/possible, show interest in your host's background, education, family, hobbies etc. Give information about your own if asked. This is part of the sharing of information which helps to build up a relationship. No need to go over the top. But it does no harm to indulge in some well-placed flattery.

- Then, after you and your interlocutor have made your respective introductory statements, make your sales pitch. Decide what are the five or six crucial points you want to get across. There is no problem about referring to a previously prepared note. Your interlocutor may well do this. It shows that you have made an effort to prepare.

- Do not be afraid of silences. Sit tight and wait for something to happen. It is a common Westerners' flaw when in the Far East to feel that silences have to be filled. In negotiations, for instance, this normally means that the Westerner ends up conceding something.

- If, on the other hand, you are on the receiving end of a barrage of detailed and apparently pointless questions, try to bear with them and answer them. This is both a sign of interest in your business and a means of testing a potential partner.

- Personal posture is important. Sit straight in chairs at meetings even if they are armchairs. Do not slump, don't cross your legs and maintain a fairly formal style. Don't blow your

26

nose noisily. Don't drink tea offered to you before your host has invited you to do so. Shake hands at the beginning and at the end of meetings.

- If you are taking gifts, make sure that they are neatly wrapped, if possible professionally. Tatty wrapping is a British disease; as are cheap gifts. They indicate a discourtesy to the recipient. Do not give the gift until the end of the meeting. Do not be fazed if you have given agift and not received one. You will have scored a point. Don't open the gift until you've left the meeting: if it is not very good, you will embarrass your host. If you open it, your host will also have to open yours and that could embarrass you!

- Accept offers of hospitality with the same grace with which they are made. Entertainment outside the office is another way in which Japanese hosts test a potential business relationship before committing themselves fully. Try to enter into the spirit of things. On taking the first drink at meals, toast your host by raising a glass to him/her and to those around you before you drink. Don't drink until these toasts take place. And if you are called on to sing - have a go! If your Japanese hosts are able to enjoy themselves singing with you, they will probably enjoy doing business with you.

Key Challenges in Japanese Market

Some of the issues to consider when doing business are covered above. Key challenges will vary according to circumstances but may include culture (especially the need for a long-term commitment and the importance of connections and personal relationships), language and long-term established business practices and relationships in some sectors.

Chapter 6: Social Interaction

Your hosts may bring up the idea of getting together socially later. This may be a sincere invitation to dinner; it may just be polite banter. Do not be offended if an invitation turns out to have been just talk and don't aggressively bug your counterpart about when you can get together. He may not say "no" directly so you might need to read from his body language what he really wants.

If you do go out for dinner, keep in mind that "going Dutch" is not normal in Japan. If you are the buyer, you'll likely be in for a free evening of entertainment. If you're the seller... well, if you were a local, you'd probably be picking up the tab. However, it's not quite this simple since your hosts may still insist on paying because you are a visitor in their country. Also, it is normal for the inviting party to pay.

In all cases, if your host is planning to bear the dinner expenses, make at least a meek attempt to pay. Don't worry... he won't let you. But even your insincere attempt to pick up the tab will have looked good. And, you can offer to pay for his dinner when he visits your home country.

Japanese are unlikely to invite you into their homes. It is normal for dinner meetings to be held in restaurants. Also, it is common to extend an evening's entertainment by going out to a coffee shop (or a second round of drinking) after the meal. If your host has paid for the meal, you might want to consider being even more pushy about paying for the coffee or drinks. But be careful! In some settings (especially where hostesses are involved), drinks can get very expensive.

Japanese are liable to ask you questions that make you uncomfortable, such as your age. You don't have to answer, but at least be gracious about it. They are certainly not trying to be offensive; it's just that some questions you would consider rude back home are not necessarily impolite in the country you are visiting.

Japanese love to drink alcohol with and after dinner. If you don't drink... well, that's a strike against you. You should try to drink. But if drinking is completely out of the question, make up an excuse and be ready to explain it several different ways and times. Your hosts may push you to drink and you should be careful not to get angry.

If alcohol is served, DO NOT drink from the bottle. You should pour the beverage into a cup or glass provided and then drink. Tipping is not customary in Japan and you don't have to do it.

When eating with your hosts, try to eat some of everything and look like you are enjoying the food. If there are certain kinds of food you don't like, it would be helpful to alert your hosts to this before they choose the restaurant or the meal. They'll appreciate hearing that you like their food.

Chapter 7: How to Invest in Japan

FDI into Japan has been historically low at 1-2% of GDP. The government recognises the need to increase this to bring in fresh blood into the Japanese economy and set a target to double this between 2001-2006. A new target to raise FDI stock against GDP to 5% by 2010 was announced in 2006 and the figure as of end 2009 stood at 3.9%. The Japan External Trade Organisation

(JETRO), whose chief function used to be to promote imports into Japan (to counter international criticism of Japanese trade surpluses in the 1980/90s), has become primarily an inward investment promotion agency. JETRO provides consultation for entry strategy to foreign companies and also a fixed term free office space in Tokyo and other major cities in Japan for foreign companies until they find a permanent location. Local governments are also welcoming of FDI and have subsidy programmes (for feasibility study or market visits to explore the possibility of investing in a specific region) and free/low cost incubation facilities.

The US is by far the largest investor in Japan, followed by European countries such as France, Germany and the Netherlands. There are more than 400 UK companies with a presence in Japan.
UK investors include Astra Zeneca, GSK, GKN, Shell, BT, Smith & Nephew, Symbian, ARM, HSBC,

Barclays Capital, RBS, Tesco, Travelex, Lush and many others.

There are no restrictions on foreign ownership of a company except for regulated business sectors such as broadcasting, telecommunications and civil aviation.

Setting up a company in Japan has become less onerous and less expensive. There is a wealth of information, including on the forms of entities and practicalities of setting them up, to be found on JETRO's "Invest Japan!" website at http://www.jetro.go.jp/en/invest/index.html

The British Industry Centre (BIC) was set up in 1998 with the aim to provide a hassle-free starting point for UK companies wishing to set up in Japan. It is located in Hodogaya, Yokohama City (45 minute train journey from central Tokyo) in a contemporary office building, Yokohama Business Park. It offers British companies affordable accommodation and communal meeting rooms and secretarial support and has been home to more than 30 British companies of which many have grown their business significantly to the extent that they needed to locate into larger offices.

Financial Assistance

TOKYO AIM is an equity market for growing international companies and is a joint venture between the Tokyo Stock Exchange and the London Stock Exchange. Their website is at www.tokyo-aim.com.

Chapter 8: Political and Economic Risk

The Democratic Party of Japan (DPJ) won a majority in the election for the House of Representatives in August 2009. They campaigned for a manifesto including governmental reform and the elimination of wasteful projects, child support policies, support to the agricultural sector and the abolition of motorway tolls. In September 2009, president of the DPJ, Yukio Hatoyama was elected as Prime Minister. However, in June 2010, Hatoyama resigned due to lack of fulfilments of his policies, both domestically and internationally and soon after, Naoto Kan succeeded the post. Kan suffered an early setback in the House of Councillors election in 2010. Despite falling popularity, Kan rejected calls to step down while the country continued to suffer from the earthquake, tsunami, and nuclear crises of 11 March 2011. With passage of three bills (second supplementary budget, bond issuance and renewable energy) which he made final conditions for his departure, Kan finally resigned in August 2011 after just over a year in office.

DPJ's new president and former finance minister of Kan's cabinet, Yoshihiko Noda was cleared and elected by the Diet as 95th Prime Minister (Japan's sixth new Prime Minister in five years) on 30 August 2011. The formation of a new government offers some glimmer of hope of more stable governance. A low-key pragmatist and deficit hawk, Noda has restored some authority to the bureaucracy, tried to forge party unity and sought to cooperate with the oppositions. In his policy speech, Noda signalled a strong sense of continuity with the policies of the preceding Kan government. Noda said that reconstruction would be his government's top priority. The government would prepare a new growth strategy by the end of the year and a new energy policy by summer 2012 to address the impact of the March 2011 disaster and radiation crisis on the economy. He promised to restart nuclear plants following safety checks, but also echoed in general terms Kan's pledge to reduce Japan's reliance on nuclear energy over the long term.

After two months since his appointment, Noda is still relatively highly regarded among both public and bureaucrats. His current support rate has slipped but is still about 50%. Senior officials speak well of him, which is different from recent prime ministers. However, PM Noda has various challenges in front of him to drive forward a sustainable recovery. Such challenges include the TPP (Trans-Pacific Partnership) negotiations and tax increases for financing reconstruction efforts. The fate of the administration could hinge on its ability to achieve these goals.

Chapter 9: Bribery and Corruption

Bribery is illegal and has no place in British business, at home or abroad. It is an offence for UK nationals and bodies incorporated under UK law to bribe anywhere in the world. From 01 July 2011 the Bribery Act makes it an offence for commercial organisations carrying on a business in the UK to fail to prevent bribery on their behalf by employees and other associated persons.

UK enforcement is increasing, with a number of UK nationals and companies recently fined or imprisoned for their involvement in overseas corruption.

Overseas corruption also hurts honest companies and raises the costs of doing business. Surveys regularly show that a significant number of UK companies have lost business to a bribing competitor or turned down overseas opportunities due to overseas corruption.

The UK is working with our peers at the OECD, UN and other international bodies to level the global playing field and confront local cultures of corruption.

The UN has recently launched a new initiative called Tools and Resources for Anti-Corruption Knowledge (TRACK). This includes a legal library containing laws, jurisprudence and other information on anti-corruption authorities from over 175 States worldwide, indexed and searchable according to each provision of the UN Convention Against Convention (e.g. official embezzlement, prohibitions against bribery, procurement, etc).

In addition, a commercial organisation carrying on a business in the UK can be liable for the conduct of a person who is neither a UK national or resident in the UK or a body incorporated or formed in the UK. In this case it does not matter whether the acts or omissions which form part of the offence take place in the UK or elsewhere.

In 2010 Japan was ranked joint 17, with the United Kingdom, out of 180 countries in Transparency International's corruption perception index (CPI) and received a "strong" rating in the 2008 Global Integrity Index. It lags behind many western countries however in terms of civil service governance and anti-corruption law, and in public procurement and whistleblower protection. Business gifts are exchanged in Japan much more than in Europe, and this can cause unease among newcomers to the Japanese market.

Bribery Act 2010

The Bribery Act 2010 came into force on 01 July 2011 and, following extensive consultation with business, has published the Bribery Act guidance. The intention of the guidance is to provide commercial organisations with the information they need to put in place to prevent bribery on their behalf. Alongside the full guidance, there is also a quick start guide which it is hoped will be particularly useful to SMEs.

The Director of the Serious Fraud Office and the Director of Public Prosecutions have published guidance on their approach to prosecutorial decision-making in respect of offences under the Act. During the consultation period, there was particular interest in a number of areas:

Hospitality and Promotional Expenditure - The Bribery Act does not prohibit hospitality, and the Ministry of Justice guidance confirms that hospitality is allowed as long as it is reasonable and proportionate. The independent prosecution authority guidance confirms that excessively lavish hospitality is an important consideration in the decision on whether to prosecute. Other public interest factors include whether the hospitality was not clearly connected with a legitimate business activity, or was concealed.

Facilitation payments – UK law has never provided an exemption for facilitation payments (small bribes to secure routine government action). The Bribery Act does not change that position. We believe they also undermine corporate anti-bribery procedures and confuse the anti-bribery message to employees and business partners. The Ministry of Justice guidance makes clear that payments specifically permitted or required under local law are not bribes (e.g. as part of a transparent fast-track scheme for business visas). The Ministry of Justice guidance also makes clear that, where payments are made in response to immediate threats to life or limb, the general common law defence of duress may be available.

Furthermore, the independent prosecution authority guidance makes clear that they will have regard to the public interest in prosecution of facilitation payments particularly where they are paid, for example, where the payer was in a vulnerable position because of the circumstances where the payment was demanded (e.g. demands by armed militia at roadblocks).

Chapter 10: Organised Crime and Human Rights

Japan has a number of organised crime syndicates, yakuza. These groups tend to operate in the entertainment and construction industries in particular. Companies operating in Japan should be prepared for approaches from the yakuza and develop appropriate contingency plans.

Human Rights

The Government believes that free trade and economic growth promote development and respect for human rights. We encourage British businesses to be aware of their potential impacts on human rights. Through the FCO human rights webpage you will see information for businesses that operate, or intend to operate, in countries where there are human rights concerns.

As British business expands overseas I encourage you to ensure that this success is not achieved at the expense of human rights. You should strive to promote competitive and transparent conditions for doing business by spreading internationally agreed standards of responsible business and best practice. Good business and respect for human rights should be mutually reinforcing. Respect for human rights helps legitimate, sustainable business; it creates stable operating environments and sustainable markets with lessened risk of reputational damage or of litigation.

And good business practice has a positive impact on human rights; it sets standards of behaviour, improves governance, provides livelihoods free of abuse, removes incentives to abuse, helps tackle disadvantage, maximises skills and sustainable employability and strengthens communities.

Protect your people, your information and your skills

Protective security advice is aimed at reducing the vulnerability of your business and staff to national security threats, including those such as terrorism, cyber attack or espionage.

The most effective way to secure your business against these is to use a combination of measures covering physical, personnel and information security; including cyber security.

Almost every business relies on the confidentiality, integrity and availability of its data. Protecting information, whether it is held electronically or by other means, should be at the heart of the organisation's security planning

Cyber crime in the "virtual" environment is today the world's fastest-growing crime sector. Your cyber security is paramount if you are beginning to trade overseas or expanding your overseas business.

CPNI provides a range of guidance documents and technical notes aimed at improving practices and raising awareness of current issues related to information security.

Such measures can defend against electronic attack, instil good practice processes, improve process control, and system security alike.
Physical security

Physical security is important in protecting against a range of threats and addressing vulnerability. You should put in place security measures to remove or reduce your vulnerabilities to as low as reasonably practicable, bearing in mind the need to consider safety as a priority at all times.

Advice on Physical security measures is provided on ways to protect buildings, contents, equipment and so on. These include basic good housekeeping, CCTV/intruder alarms/access control systems, parking and traffic controls, mail screening and lighting.

Personnel security

Personnel security is a system of policies and procedures which seek to manage the risk of staff or contractors exploiting their legitimate access to an organisation's assets or premises for unauthorised purposes. These purposes can encompass many forms of criminal activity, from minor theft through to terrorism.

The CPNI website includes guidance on how such risks, including those from "insiders", can be minimised. It also covers pre-employment screening, personal document verification, security culture, on-going personnel security measures and personnel risk assessments.

How to guard against organised crime risks

UK business is at risk of being targeted and exploited by serious organised criminals, with the potential loss from fraud and money laundering alone running into billions of pounds every year.

The first step towards combating organised crime and reducing its impact on the UK is to understand the various threats involved.

The UK's Serious Organised Crime Agency, or SOCA works with the private sector to improve understanding of the threats faced by industry and shares information to help protect UK businesses. SOCA's reach extends internationally.

SOCA's annual UK threat assessment from serious organised crime describes and weighs-up threats posed to the UK by serious organised criminals.

This, along with further related information on protecting your business from organised crime, is available from the SOCA website.

SOCA can also advise you about reporting suspicious activities such as money-laundering or drug trafficking.

Please note: SOCA does not have a public information line about its activities and it is not a crime-reporting agency.

Chapter 11: Intellectual Property

Your company's intellectual property may be its most valuable asset. Intellectual property, or IP, is any form of original creation that can be bought or sold, from music to machinery. When you're doing business overseas, you need to keep it secure.

There are many simple and cost effective ways of protecting your ideas and your business.

IP exists in four main forms: patents, trademarks, designs and copyright.

- Patents protect the processes that make things work.
- Trademarks protect logos that distinguish goods and services.
- Designs protect the look of three-dimensional shapes.
- Copyright protects material only when it is written down or recorded. Each provides different ways with which to guard your property.

Key information on how to protect your IP abroad, is available from the Intellectual Property Office. It offers various forms of support and advises on all four main forms: patent protection abroad, trademarks abroad, designs protection abroad and copyright abroad.

The World Intellectual Property Organisation (WIPO), website includes information from 184

Member States on membership of the different WIPO treaties; national IP legislation; contact details of IP Offices; country profile, and more.

Chapter 12: Understanding the Market

There are eight economic regions in Japan, with the top 3 regions being Kanto (surrounding Tokyo), Kinki (surrounding Osaka) and Chubu (surrounding Nagoya). Japan's current population is 127 million.

Distribution and Sales Channels

Direct Sale

This may not be recommended since the Japanese market can be complicated, and customers (no matter if wholesaler, dealer, end-user...etc.) may ask for detailed and elaborate service, delivery and/or high quality product.

Japanese Distributor

Most recommended for U.S. and European firms. This allows the manufacturer to build on the expertise and client base of an established Japanese firm.

Agent/Representative

Good during the business's start-up period in Japan and/or if the U.S. and European company should have specific or solid customer(s) in Japan already, etc.

Wholesaler

In Japan, some wholesalers may be a good candidate for a business partner since they have a strong distribution channel and network. Others may not be appropriate since they may be tied to specific customers (particularly to manufacturers in the same industry) and would not accept competitor's products from overseas.

Franchising

No barriers to the franchising of any product or service in Japan. If it is a very good and popular franchise business in the U.S. and European, it will have good potential in Japan as well.

U.S. and European companies that want to establish a presence in Japan should carefully select the appropriate type of corporation. This determines their tax obligations, other liabilities and the operations they are allowed to perform in Japan. The procedure for establishing a presence in Japan is different depending on what type of entity will be established, whether it is a representative office, branch office or domestic company in Japan, etc.

Due Diligence

Due diligence is essential before entering any type of agreement in Japan. Keep the following points in mind when choosing a Japanese business partner:

- Product and industry knowledge, track record, enthusiasm and commitment should be weighted heavily.
- Personally interview potential candidates at their home offices.
- Provide appropriate training, product support and timely supply of spare parts and keep up with a sufficient and punctual delivery service/system.
- Obtain information from a local consulting or law firm or local business chamber. The Japanese legal system is different from the U.S. and European system (depending on items).

Pricing a Product
- Pay special attention to import duties, brokers' fees, transportation costs and taxes as well as existing products' pricing to determine if the product/service can be priced competitively.
- There are some products from overseas that are not subject to Japanese custom duty/fee.
- Payment terms and financing costs also make a difference in the pricing structure.

Essential Factors for Success
- High quality products at competitive prices.
- Financing, delivery, brand name recognition, before and after sales support and customer service.
- Efficient business culture.

- Strong personal relationships in all Japanese business transactions.

Import Requirements

In Japan, import requirements and/or regulations are very different depending on each product and/or industry. The authority which oversees each product or industry is different. It is highly recommended to research each item/product and/or to look for an appropriate importer that already has or will be able to obtain import licenses for each item/product in concern.

Government Procurement

The Agreement on Government Procurement, which went into effect in January 1981, sets forth rules for non-discrimination between foreign and domestic sources and for the treatment same as Japanese nationals. This Agreement was subsequently reviewed on a number of occasions, and as a result of negotiations concurrent to those of the Uruguay Round, the Agreement was amended.

- To broaden the scope of government procurement (applying to regional governments, and to a broader range of government-related entities).
- To apply the Agreement to the procurement of services.
- To introduce a complaint review system pertaining to procurement procedures. This Agreement, signed by 23 countries, went into effect on January 1, 1996.

Chapter 13: Key Policy Updates Post Earthquake

Overseas M&As by cash-rich Japanese companies continue to increase because of the strong Yen and Japanese banks are expanding their overseas business: – For example, Sumitomo Mitsui Banking Corporation announced a tie up with a Mexican bank, Scotiabank Inverlat, S.A. whose parent is The Bank of Nova Scotia in Canada, to provide fund settlement services in Mexican peso to support Japanese firms investing in Mexico.

Corporate Governance has remained a hot topic. The entire board of Olympus has announced it will resign and a new management will be set up in mid February 2012, following recent revelations of a cover up of earlier loses An independent committee will monitor the firm's corporate governance and compliance. The Legislative Council under the Minister of Justice, plans to submit proposals to reform the Companies Act next year in response to increased questions about the credibility of Japanese corporate governance.

Tax and social security reform – The Government's Tax Committee, chaired by Finance Minister Azumi, has been considering plans for tax and social security reform and an internal DPJ Tax Committee is also likely to play a significant role. They are likely to finalise their plans in mid December 2011 and to start discussions with the opposition parties from January

2012. The Government plans to submit bills, including the consumption tax hike, to the Diet in 2012 Q1 but would not introduce the tax until after a future election, which must be held at the latest in summer 2013. (The DPJ in their 2009 election manifesto said it would not raise consumption tax during the life time of the parliament).

The Government has previously indicated that it would like to increase consumption tax from 5% to 10% by the mid 2010s, but this proposal is not universally accepted. Some ministries are requesting there are relief measures for certain products and services such as home acquisitions to avoid a fall off in demand. However, the Senior MoF Vice Minister Igarashi has indicated that such exemptions should only be considered after the consumption tax rate is raised to 10%.

FY2012 tax reform - Separately, the Government's Tax Committee also finalised the outline of FY2012 tax reforms. On the whole, it is viewed as a package that is trying to placate those who are opposed to a consumption tax hike by alleviating tax in those areas where there are concerns that demand might fall. A cut in the automobile weight tax will be reduced by JPY150bn (GBP1.2bn) in FY2012 and further cuts will be made from FY2013 onwards and the removal or reduction of automobile acquisition tax is also under discussion. The automobile industry however would like further measures. Tax breaks for acquiring environmentally-friendly houses are also included. The Government has also included the introduction of an environment tax which will raise taxes on petroleum and coal by 150%, and this is expected to provoke a huge reaction from the opposition in the next Diet Session from January 2012.

Tax hike for reconstruction – The bill to raise tax for reconstruction purposes passed the Diet in late November 2011 alongside the third supplementary budget (JPY12tr, 2% of GDP). It includes:

- Increasing income tax for 25 years by 2.1%.
- Increasing residential tax for 10 years.
- Reducing corporate tax by only approximately 2.7% (net) for three years instead of the planned 5% cut.

Fourth supplementary budget – PM Noda announced that the government will bring forward a fourth supplementary budget in FY2011. The size is expected to be around JPY2.5tr (GBP21bn, 0.5% of GDP) and the bill is likely to be submitted to the Diet in January 2012. This package will include support for the agricultural sector because of concerns about joining TPP negotiations and a JPY300bn (GBP2.5bn) subsidy for the purchase of environmentally-friendly cars ('eco-cars'), which successfully boosted the demand for cars from June 2009 to September 2010. It will be financed without any new JGB issuance as debt servicing costs have been lower than expected securing a 'saving' of JPY1tr (GBP8.2bn) and tax receipts have been higher than expected generating approximately JPY1tr (GBP8.2bn) of additional revenue.

Monetary Policy – BoJ kept its policy rate unchanged at 0-0.1%. There was a coordinated action among major central banks on 30th November 2011 to provide liquidity support to the global financial system. In addition the BoJ has subsequently provided $4.77 billion to money markets in order to help cover any of year end funding difficulties.

There is concern that USD funding pressure may becoming a problem in the region. In response to the exposure of the Korean market to European banks. Japanese authorities have set up a $70bn USD swap facility with the Bank of Korea.

Trade Policy – EU/Japan had the third scoping exercise talks regarding the Economic Partnership Agreement (EPA) and some progress was made. EU/Japan aims at producing a scoping report in January / February 2012 which if accepted may lead to the start of actual negotiations in May/June 2012. The Japanese government has now put together a negotiating team to take forward work on the TPP but there continue to be significant opposition to entry; a recent poll indicated half of the population were in favour but a third against. Elsewhere, Japan/Korea/China FTA negotiations are reportedly making a progress, and may start as early as summer 2012. Japan has also reopened stalled FTA negotiations with Australia.

Japanese direct exposure to the Eurozone crisis is not at a level which would be significantly damaging. Europe accounts for about 10% of total exports and Japanese banks do not have substantial exposure to Eurozone sovereign debt. Where the Japanese banks do have exposure we are seeing some transfer to JGBs.

Japan is however more concerned about secondary effects; for example from a slowdown in global trade or the impact on money markets. The Japanese authorities have taken a 20% stake in European Financial Stability Fund (EFSF) bonds and have indicated that they will be prepared to take further action but on condition that the Europeans take further measures first.

Chapter 14: Doing Business in Japan after the Earthquake

Since the earthquake and tsunamis on the 11th of March 2011 and the nuclear problems, I am sure this is all you have seen and heard a lot about Japan in the media. As with all such events in the world, we think there have been some inaccuracies in the reporting and on occasions a lack of detail. I hope this book will correct some of those errors and also fill in the gaps.

Today it is safe to visit and conduct business in Japan. Business is getting back to normal–Impacts and opportunities?

On 11 March 2011, the fourth largest earthquake on record hit Northeast Japan, the region called Tohoku. Combined by the subsequent tsunamis and Fukushima Nuclear Plant problems, it has become the most expensive natural disaster in history, with an initial estimated cost of up to £190 billion, which is between 3 to 5% of GDP.

This does not mean that the whole country was destroyed. Although there are ongoing serious relief, recovery and reconstruction operations in the affected regions, business activities have never stopped in other regions and in some way in the affected regions too.

Today, it is safe to visit Japan, eat the food and drink the water. Western Japan, has in fact never been significantly affected including travel restrictions. Business is pretty much back to normal, with many Japanese companies having recovered their operations completely or found alternative suppliers, locations and so on. Some foreign companies temporarily relocated their operations, but almost all have come back to Tokyo. Therefore, Tokyo is very much back to its usual busy, hectic and vibrant feel. Other than some evidence of power saving such as office temperatures slightly higher, some escalators closed or electric signs switched off, it is hard to see real evidence of 11.3 around Tokyo.

So, what are the real impacts and what opportunities do we now have for British exports? I would like to start with an overview of the Japanese economy in the next chapter.

Chapter 15: Overview of Japanese Economy after the Earthquake

Japan is the third largest economy in the world, after the United States and China. Japan has recently fallen behind China in GDP terms and growth is much faster in China; However, GDP per capital is still 10 times that of China and Japan has a much higher quality business environment. One crucial long term challenge for Japan is its ageing and declining population, projected to be 117 million people in 2030, down from its current figure of 127 million.

This is just to quickly show the size of the Japanese economy in terms of GDP. For example, the Kanto region which includes Tokyo is the same size as Russia, the Kansai region which includes the second largest city Osaka is the same size as Netherlands.

UK' total trade with Japan; both exports and imports in 2009 was £18 billion. Out of this, exports to Japan account for £8.1 billion and imports from Japan for £9.9 billion. For the UK, Japan is the largest export market outside of Europe and the US, although it is likely that China is now a larger export market.

Despite the Lehman crisis, financial services continue to be the biggest UK export to Japan, accounting for nearly 35%. Medical and pharmaceutical products, power generating machinery and equipment and travel services remain to be key export sectors. Latest figures show that a combined figure of machinery and transport equipment is made up 36% and chemicals and related products 30%.

Japan"s steady recovery path from the Lehman crisis was suddenly disrupted by the earthquake. The January-March GDP fell by 0.9% quarter-on-quarter. This push Japan back into a technical recession (in Q1 2011).

However, both the authorities and private sector analysts expect a recovery from the third quarter, i.e., sometime between July and September. Manufacturers are making their best efforts to restore their production lines and expect to resume normal operation in Autumn. The general view is that Japan will come back to its recovery path by the end of this year.

There are two big negative impacts for industries. One is the "supply chain disruption". Auto and semiconductor industries were the most affected since 20% of the products or parts were produced in the Tohoku area. Factories suspended operations and production has suffered worldwide disruptions due to a shortage of parts. In fact, here in the UK, Japanese automotive manufacturers have had to scale back on production.

The other major impact has been a power shortage. The accidents at Fukushima Nuclear Plant located 150miles northeast of Tokyo reduced and delayed business investment and supply. The ongoing repair efforts have not yet managed to settle problems and the Government has announced a 15% power cut in the summer, initially in northeast Japan and Tokyo.

A similar 10-15% measurement is likely to spread nationwide as the result of the post-earthquake safety-check inspections required by the government. Industries and individual businesses have started considering measures to minimise the impact by, for example, introducing summer time and rotational operation of plants.

Chapter 16: Earthquake Impact on GDP was more Significant

The revised GDP data revealed that the earthquake hit Japan's economy harder than had previously been thought. But the post earthquake recovery has still been significant. Global economic slowdown also has adverse effect.

The impact of the Eurozone crisis and the Thai floods became apparent in October 2011 economic data. Exports fell to all destinations and the production outlook has become weaker due to growing uncertainty.

Yen stood firm as a 'safe haven' currency

The Japanese Yen traded strongly against all major currencies which continue to have impact on exports. But the currency market is cautious about further Government intervention and although the USD/JPY was strong it was fairly stable.

Consumption tax debate

PM Noda plans to set out his plans for the tax and social security reform before Christmas with aim of putting in place legislation in Q1 2012 but the tax would not be introduced until after a future election.

Revised quarterly GDP data showed larger than expected immediate earthquake shock The Cabinet Office (CAO) announced a revised set of quarterly

GDP figures which showed that in the aftermath of the earthquake Japan's real GDP was more significantly affected than had originally been calculated. The revised real GDP growth figures for Q1, Q2 and Q3 are -1.7%, -0.5% and 1.4% while the original figures were -0.7%, -0.3% and 1.5%; the change is likely to reflect a massive fall in inventories..

Business investment in Q3 was revised down as were private and public consumption figures, but upward revisions to public investment, inventories and exports almost offset these changes.

Private sector forecasts for FY2011 (currently +0.4% on average) are likely to be revised down and the CAO and the Bank of Japan (BoJ) is also likely to revise their forecasts in late December (CAO, currently +0.5%) and late January (BoJ, currently +0.3%). But there are no significant changes expected, at least for now, for FY2012 and FY2013 (2.0% and 1.4% respectively), since it is widely believed that the economy has almost recovered from the impact of the earthquake although of course global developments are likely to have an impact.

Global economic slowdown is creating anxiety

Authorities revised down their overall economic assessments in November 2011 due to the slowdown in the global economy. CAO and BoJ both stated that "the Japanese economy is recovering from the earthquake but at a moderate pace". In addition to the power supply issues as a result of the close down of nuclear plants, the negative impacts of the Eurozone crisis and the Thai floods have started to become apparent. And in the short term the Thai flooding has had the biggest impact.

Industrial production in October 2011 was stronger than expected (+2.4% month-on-month, 95% of the pre-earthquake level). Although the production of electronic parts and devices and ICT equipment fell sharply, there were strong results in transport and general machinery. Thailand is Japan's key production partner in the auto sector, importing parts from Japan, assembling them to produce the final products and exporting to other countries. In the shorter term the effects of the Thai floods on auto production are likely to continue. And this will have a knock on impact on sales and therefore Japan's income balance.

Due to the Thai floods, weakening global demand and the strong Yen, exports in October 2011 fell and Japan's trade deficit (seasonally adjusted) widened again, falling into the red for the seventh straight month. Exports to all destinations shrank and exports of electrical and general machinery fell sharply. There were increased imports of LNG (liquefied natural gas) and crude oil for supplying thermal power plants as they substitute for the reduced nuclear power capacity. In December 2011 only 6 out of the 54 nuclear plants will be operating; in November 2011 it was ten.

The domestic household sector remained solid in October 2011. Household consumption was flat and retail sales rose for the first time in 4 months. While the demand for TVs continued to fall (after the full transition to digital broadcasting in July 2011), demand for other items such as clothes, general merchandise and drugs and toiletry products increased month-on-month. However, private consumption in Q4 (October-December 2011) is expected to slow down as consumer sentiment gradually weakens in response to the uncertain global economic situation as well as concerns about possible tax hikes.

The labour market situation was mixed. The unemployment rate in October 2011 rose to 4.5% from 4.1% in September 2011, and the data indicates that those who withdrew from the labour market after the earthquake have started to return to look for jobs.

Deflation continued due to the ongoing negative demand-supply gap as well as the appreciation of the Yen. Core CPI (excluding fresh foods) and "core core" CPI (excluding fresh foods and energy) in October were -0.1% and -1.0% (year-on-year) respectively. With the BoJ revising down their CPI forecasts in October for FY2011 and FY2012 to 0.0% and +0.1% (from +0.7% for both years in July), the deflationary trend is expected to persist on the back of growing concerns about the global economic slowdown and financial market stress.

Chapter 17: Healthcare and Medical Devices in Japan

Japan is the world's second largest market for both healthcare and medical devices. With nearly 50% of medical devices being imported, Japan is open to innovative and high quality products and technologies.

Japan is the world's 2nd largest market in terms of government's expenditures on healthcare. The Japanese Government spent £38.7 billion in FY 2009, which was about 10% of Japan's GDP. The healthcare spending is expected to see a further increase as the ageing problem develops. In 2010, 23.1% of the 127 million Japanese population were over 65 years old. This is forecasted to increase to over 30.5% in 2025.

Japan is also the second largest market in the world for medical devices. It was worth ¥2.2 trillion (approx £18.3 billion) in 2009 when the market for imports of medical devices alone was approximately £8 billion.

Medical services are provided in a free access system, in which citizens can choose any medical institution throughout Japan. Therefore, even patients with a mild illness tend to visit a large hospital equipped with various high tech instruments/devices. This is in marked contrast to the UK, where the first point of call is likely to be the GP.

Japan has one of the world's fastest growing elderly populations. As of September 2010, approximately 23.1% of Japan's 127 million people are over 65 and this figure is anticipated to increase to 30.5% by 2025 and to 40.5% by 2055.

Japan has relatively strong manufacturing capabilities for diagnostic equipment, including CT, MRI and Electrocardiography, supplied by some globally known manufacturers including Toshiba Medical Systems, Olympus Medical Systems and Hitachi Medico. In 2009, imports of medical devices made up nearly half the market (49.4%). Of all foreign suppliers, the US retained more than half of that share with 53.3%.

The UK is increasing its share steadily from 1.3% in 2004 to 2.3% in 2009 and was positioned as Japan's eighth largest foreign supplier of medical devices in 2009. The top three categories for imports were as follows:

- Artificial internal organ apparatus and assistive devices (32.6%).
- General surgical/orthopaedic supplies and related products (23%).
- Ophthalmic devices and products

Key opportunities

For the healthcare market, unique, sophisticated, fashionable and high-technology products are sought to assist elderly people, including those who are healthy, and those with disabilities.

For the medical devices market, opportunities exist for advanced and innovative products especially in the following areas:

First tier

- Diagnostics systems and equipment
- Novel medical treatments (e.g. minimally- or non-invasive surgery)
- Preventative healthcare

e-Health

Main therapeutic areas are oncology, cardiology, CNS, orthopaedics and age related diseases.

Second tier

- Diagnostics products and technologies for stratified medicine
- Surgical navigation (e.g. surgical robotics)
- Regenerative medicine

The size of the pharmaceutical market and the medical devices market is also the world's 2nd largest, worth £65 billion and £16 billion in 2009 respectively. In 2009, about a quarter of drugs available in Japan were imported. There is no official statistics about the value of technology in-licensing and M&A; however, active collaboration between Japanese and overseas drug manufacturers has been taking place to generate a huge income to overseas companies.

The UK Life Sciences industry will definitely want to capitalise on the opportunities the world's 2nd largest market offers. Japanese pharmaceutical companies have a serious and keen interest in identification of promising drug pipelines, DDS and Biomarker for in-licensing purposes and also in R&D collaboration to accelerate drug development speed. Cancer, CNS and cardiovascular are core therapeutic areas to many of the Japanese pharmaceutical companies.

Japan is generally known as a technology oriented country, but in the case of medical devices, there is room for further development of the domestic industry. The market is open to overseas products and imported products account for nearly 50% of the whole market. "Innovative" is a key word to attract the attention of Japanese companies. "Me-too" products have little opportunity. In view of the Japanese regulatory procedures, products with an FDA approval and/or of lower medical class will have larger chances to get in to the market.

The Life Sciences industry may probably be the least affected industry by the earthquake. Even companies with a production base near the epicentre resumed business relatively soon after the crisis by shifting the production base to other locations.

Finding good and loyal, local business partners is the key for both the healthcare and medical devices markets, rather than direct market entry. Medical devices are regulated under the Pharmaceutical Affairs Law in Japan and local companies will be able to assist with regulatory issues and guide you through the best possible route into the market.

Japanese companies attach great importance in developing trust and mutual confidence that will lead to a strong and enduring relationship.

Chapter 18: Energy sector in Japan

Japan is embarking on a large shift in the make-up of its energy-mix, with reform in the electricity sector and more use of renewables, offering opportunities to UK companies with expertise.

Japan is a developed market now looking at renewable energy as a serious provider following the events of March 2011. It is looking to embark on major shift in the make-up of the energy-mix and is aiming at a 25% target of renewable energy (offshore wind, solar PV and biomass).

Japan has 54 nuclear reactors, of which 52 are currently offline. Japan's energy needs will peak in the summer and a shortfall is expected.

Japan is also looking at electricity sector reform (generation and distribution); this may offer potential opportunities to UK business. There is strong interest in Smart-Grid and Smart metering technology from utility companies.

Japan is currently importing large volumes of LNG for power generation.

Key opportunities
- Management of renewable programmes.
- Expertise on Smart-Grid/Smart Meters.
- Emergency power generation.

Chapter 19: Advanced Engineering Sector in Japan

Major opportunities for UK companies in the Advanced Engineering sector with strong credentials in innovative low carbon technology.

Advanced Engineering is a broad sector including marine, aerospace, automotive, mechanical engineering and process engineering, metallurgical process plant, metals, minerals and materials, and mining and other engineering fields.

Recent work has centred around heavy machine, machine tools and the automotive and auto sport areas. Japanese companies continue to look for high quality proven technologies for applications for use in both domestic and International projects.

I will focus on the automotive sector because of its importance both domestically and globally.

The March earthquake could not have struck at a worse time for the Japanese automotive industry. Like all the other major vehicle making countries, Japan had been feeling the effects of the global downturn in the industry. Japan's gross exports and imports decreased in 2009 by 33% and 35% respectively over the previous year.

The disaster had a devastating effect on the supply chain of all the automotive companies since a lot of the parts suppliers were located in the Tohoku region.

However, recovery has been faster than anticipated and in the case of Toyota, they expect their car production levels to be 70% of where it was pre-disaster from June onwards. Other manufacturers are in a similar situation.

But it is not all doom and gloom - there are opportunities. With the global drive to reduce carbon emissions from transport, Japan, as one of the world's leading automotive nations, is urgently seeking to respond to that challenge, thereby creating an opportunity for high-tech exports. In 1998 Japan's Energy Conservation Law recommended vehicle fuel efficiency targets for fiscal year 2010. Alternative energy vehicles which run on power or fuels such as electricity, natural gas and diesel alternative LPG are becoming increasingly popular owing to their significantly reduced CO_2 and other tailpipe emissions.

Japanese companies regard UK automotive technology companies as world leaders in the field of low carbon. Unfortunately, there has been a lack of opportunities for technical exchange. Even if Japanese car manufacturers have a manufacturing base in the UK, UK automotive technology companies need to establish contact with the HQs in Japan to explore business opportunities.

Key opportunities
- Low carbon vehicles
- Emergency Power Generation
- Earthquake safety equipment

Chapter 20: Food and Drink Sector in Japan

This market was least hit by the earthquake although hotels and restaurants in Tokyo are still struggling. A wide variety of many British products have been imported into Japan for many years now, including an increase in organic products in recent years.

Consumers have become more and more conscious about food safety. Likewise, "natural" and "healthy" are attractive key words. A successful British example is the soft drinks brand Firefly, which is sold 5 times more expensive than ordinary Japanese soft drinks but selling well to working women. This could also be an example of petite luxury.

Japan has high levels of consumption, and food and drink (eating out, at home and take away) makes up a significant proportion of spending. The market is very sophisticated and ready to appreciate high-quality, unique products from overseas.

Although traditional local culinary culture remains, Japanese consumers have enjoyed diverse food products which are now available at supermarkets, department stores, grocers and even convenience stores. The Japanese also value the country of origin and stories behind products. Authentic products including black teas, whiskies, biscuits/shortbread and Scottish smoked salmon have been the most popular British products in the market while olive oils and pasta sauces, which may not be easily linked to the UK, may find market entry more difficult.

The Japanese also attach significant importance on packaging and presentation. Overseas companies are sometimes requested to make special arrangements for the Japanese market.

Key opportunities

UKTI in Japan has carried out the "A Taste of Britain" campaign for over five years in order to introduce a wide range of British products into the market, and in order to change and improve perceptions of British food amongst Japanese people.

The product categories they have found prospects for include:

- Beverages (cordials and wines)
- Biscuits / snacks / chocolates
- Teas
- Speciality foods
- Organic foods
- Sausages and bacon

In general, any type of food can be imported as long as it has been guaranteed safe for human consumption. Imported foods must undergo specified procedures at the time of import in order to verify their safety. You can find translations of Japanese food-related laws and regulations on the Japan External Trade Organisation (JETRO) website www.jetro.go.jp/en/reports/regulations/

Chapter 21: Financial Services Sector in Japan

Japan is one of the largest financial services markets in the world. Japan Post Bank is the world's largest bank in deposit terms and the country is home to three of the world's top 20 banks.

A large market with vast accumulation of personal financial assets estimated at approximately ¥1400 trillion (USD17 trillion @ $1= ¥83.15).

The top 50 institutional investors have over USD12 trillion worth of assets

Japan is home to many large pension funds, e.g. Government Pension Investment Fund with USD1400 billion which is the world's largest public pension fund.

The deposit taking and lending market is still largely occupied by the large Japanese financial institutions. Japan Post Bank is the world's largest deposit taking institution with a total asset of ¥226 trillion (£1.5 trillion) and Japan is home to three of the world's top 20 banks. Most international banks have a presence in Japan, e.g. Citibank, HSBC, Barclays and UBS but their activities tend to be more corporate customer focused. Citibank and HSBC are the only foreign banks with high-street retail banking businesses.

Japanese non-life insurance market is about USD100 billion of which more than 80% is occupied by domestic players, e.g. Tokio Marine.

Key opportunities

Asset management – Both Japanese individual savers and institutional investors are interested in investment products which give a respectable level of return against a moderate risk profile. Japanese financial institutions have been entering into alliances with several well-known UK asset management companies to enhance their offering to their clients. Japanese corporate pension funds have been pioneering investment in alternative investments including hedge funds and there are several funds with over 10% of their assets allocated to alternative investment.

Cross border M&A activities – With the saturation of the domestic market and the strength of the yen, Japanese companies are looking for growth prospects overseas and have been very active in making acquisitions. The total value of outbound M&A transactions by Japan reached ¥3 trillion between April and September 2011 alone. This trend is expected to continue and even expand into SMEs.

CFD Trading – This has been a growing area in response to some of the more finance-savvy risk taking individuals, dubbed as "Mrs Watanabe". It is expected to reach ¥800 billion (£6.6 billion) in 2012.

The Financial Services Agency (FSA) is Japan's supervisory body for the industry and there are regulations governing each strand of financial services activity. Generally speaking, it is a requirement to have a Japanese incorporation and an FSA license for the specific line of business that the company wishes to engage with. However, there are ways for working in partnership arrangement with Japanese companies with legitimate licenses if you are not providing your product/service directly to the end Japanese investor.

The Japanese stock market hit a year-low in late November 2011 due to further concerns about the Eurozone crisis. Although the market initially reacted positively to the latest announcement from the EU on strengthening fiscal discipline, market participants have since appeared not to have been convinced and are looking for more decisive solutions. The Japanese stock market is likely to mirror global stock markets. The Japanese credit market was also weak following the nervous stock market trend.

Amid the uncertainties, the Yen has continued to be a 'safe haven' against all major currencies, but the USD/JPY rate has remained stable at about 77 yen as investors are wary about further intervention by the Japanese Government. Finance Minister Azumi has continued to signal that the Government is prepared to intervene again should they notice any speculative rate change. The Euro and the Pound weakened against the Dollar the EUR/JPY and GBP/JPY have both weakened by 5% since early November 2011.

Japanese Government Bonds (JGB) continued to be a 'safe haven' asset for investors. Japanese banks, who hold over 45% of all JGBs and whose share of JGBs in their portfolio exceeds 60%, have started replacing European sovereign debt with further JGB holdings. The latest 10-year JGB bond yield is near a historical low at around 1.01%.

Reconstruction plans by the Japanese governments are scheduled to be finalized in August or September 2012.

PFI financing

Japan"s aggregate personal financial wealth amounts to approximately £10 trillion. This has traditionally been managed in a very conservative way: i.e., bank deposits with 0.01% interest rate, post bank savings or simply under the mattresses!

Whilst the majority of consumers still tend to be conservative, there is a recognition for a need for financial products that generate healthy returns as the population is aging and people need to find ways of funding life after retirement. In response to this trend, there has been an array of tie-ups between UK and Japanese financial institutions: e.g., Threadneedle Asset Management tying up with Tokio Marine Asset Management.

The bank lending market in Japan has been plateauing and the larger Japanese banks have been actively expanding their overseas business, mainly in China, ASEAN, BRICs, Middle East and North Africa. This presents opportunities for tie-ups for British companies who can provide intelligence and support to Japanese banks in these regions. Barclays and

Sumitomo Mitsui Bank have an alliance and are already seeing some synergies in this regard. Some of the larger insurance companies have been growing Islamic Insurance business in Malaysia and in the Middle East.

The large Japanese banks had limited direct exposure to the earthquake and this sector remained relatively unaffected. There is however some uncertainty as to how TEPCO will be restructured following the ensuing nuclear problem since the banks have been lending them.

There is a need for raising funds to meet the enormous reconstruction costs. Taking the deteriorating fiscal balance of Japan into account, PFI could be an attractive method. The law has been revised recently to make PFI more attractive to private sector investors by enabling segregation and sales of operation rights. There have been some reports of interest by companies in PFI opportunities in the media; however, as the Tohoku region has little track record in PFI, we need to look at this carefully.

Chapter 22 Information Technology Sector in Japan

Like the automotive industry, ICT industry both domestically and globally saw their businesses severely impacted by the damage caused by the tsunami on suppliers. But the recovery has again been quicker than anticipated with the industry now back to more or less where it was pre-quake.

The crisis has also brought new opportunities for the ICT industry, notably smart metering and cloud-based systems. With blackouts in east Japan because of the problems at the Fukushima Plant, this has brought to the fore the importance of efficient energy management and in particular smart metering. Toshiba acquired a Swiss smart grid company Landis Gyer for £1.4 billion in May. Before the earthquake, at the end of February, the Ministry of Economy, Trade and Industry issued a report called An Energy Basic Plan. This aims to introduce smart metering to every single household in Japan by early 2020s. As a result, we expect energy and ICT companies to devote more attention to the development of smart meters in the coming years.

Cloud computing has also attracted a lot of interest within the Japanese ICT sector. Again, even prior to the earthquake, local governments were trying to replace their information systems with cloud based ones to reduce costs. The crisis has made them further realise its importance for business continuity purposes. Major ICT suppliers such as NEC and

Hitachi are seeing this as a big opportunity for the start-year of cloud systems.

Besides these crisis-led opportunities, Japanese ICT businesses are still very interested in innovative technologies. Even large companies such as Panasonic and Sony are not able to do everything themselves and dependent on collaborating with others who are able to offer unique and innovative products or services. These include software and IPR, devices and services which help improve quality and efficiency of energy management, communications and display technologies. More details are available from the ICT Team in Japan.

A few examples of UK successes in this highly competitive country are: ARM, Imagination Technologies, Cambridge Silicon Radio, Novauris and video games.

Chapter 23: Creative Sector in Japan

The importance of design has become increasingly understood and recognized by Japanese businesses. Various types of businesses have potential for collaboration with British designers. One target example is Japanese manufacturers trying to develop products in view of their global market strategy with a focus on the European market. Collaboration has increased particularly in consumer electronics, furniture, kitchen and household products and giftware. Recent case studies include mobile phones, personal computer related equipment, large play furniture, weight scales, clocks and stationery.

The earthquake has led to an increasing consciousness about disasters. Japanese businesses will be required to give greater consideration to respond to unexpected circumstances and this holds true in design too. Product development with a more flexible thinking and a new way of thinking will be necessary, which may create more opportunities for external design consultancy. "Disaster resistance", "energy saving" and "ecologically friendly" could be key words over the coming years.

Japan is the 2nd largest music market in the world. It is divided into domestic and international music and international music is around 20% of the market. As it is in other markets, the Japanese music industry is changing and facing a drop in sales. It has therefore become harder to get a licensing deal.

Image of the artist and the right fit for Japan are the key. Structurally the music industry in Japan is quite different to that in the UK, which surprises a lot of people.

I will touch upon this sub-sector in the next slide as part of the Fashion Sector, but, again, there will be an annual trade mission to Japan in November.

Chapter 24: Consumer Goods Sector in Japan

The overall retail sales in March immediately after the earthquake saw a sharp decline. This was due to various factors including consumers exercising self-restraint as a mark of respect to those who were directly affected by the disaster.

Japan has however proven resilient and the bounce back came quickly. In April, major retail outlets including department stores and shopping centres achieved better sales than the year before.

At present, there is a mixture of optimism, cautiousness and uncertainty about the prospects. However, there is an encouraging number of healthy signs of recovery and expansion.

For example:
- In Osaka, a refurbished and now larger leading department store opened in mid-April and attracted more than 160,000 consumers everyday, at least during the first 10 days. Again, in Osaka, in early May, a new shopping complex including Topshop and Topman opened and, during the first month, attracted more than 5 million consumers with over £22 million worth of sales.
- IKEA will go ahead with its plan to open its 6th store in Japan in 2012 with a floor space

of 31,000 square meters. They also plan to open another store in Tokyo in 2015.

- A leading Japanese select shop chain Urban Research will open new stores this fiscal year and expects a double digit growth.
- The luxury brand Versace will re-launch in Japan this Autumn with several stores.

So, we see more evidence to allow us to be optimistic than factors to be negative.

To succeed in this highly competitive Japanese retail market, there are some "musts" for everybody.
- High quality.
- Never late for the delivery time.
- Competitive price.
- Unique sales points such as a special story about the brand.
- Flexibility to meet Japanese needs by, for example, modifying packaging and size (Dyson is a very good example of this by developing a small size to fit standard Japanese houses which tend to be smaller than western countries) and finally but not least.
- Importance of communication and relationship-building.

While price is very important, there is a trend called "petite luxury". This means little luxury treats to get you through life or give yourself a kind of reward. We call it "retail therapy" in the UK. It could be anything from a box of luxury chocolates to a pair of Jimmy

Choo shoes, or even a little more expensive can of premium beer!

Many sectors in the retail market offer opportunities for British exports, but I will touch upon a few of the most active ones:
Gift and Household Products

Quality and design are very important. Expensive products are currently difficult. "Cute" and "feminine" could be the key for products for women. Examples of successfully established brands are Cath Kidson and Liberty and an example of a very new but already successful brand is Cabbages and Roses.

Functionality is another key as represented in kitchenware. Joseph Joseph is a very successful example. Imported kitchenware is growing due to the current trend to make life at home more enjoyable and fulfilling.

Fashion

Japan is the largest export market after Europe and the US for the British fashion industry. Japanese consumers are so demanding that it is often said that if the product satisfies Japanese consumers, it can sell anywhere in the world. Not only internationally established big brands, but also new or less-known designers can be successful in this market although it may take time.

Regardless of the earthquake, Japan continues to be an important market for British fashion: e.g., since

March, Cath Kidston has already opened 10 new stores since March and Anya Hindmarch opened her 2nd flagship store in Tokyo.

It is vital to visit the country to better understand the people and the culture and check reactions to your products.

Sports and Leisure

This market covers a wide variety of products and there are many UK brands in Japan including Brompton bicycles and Berghaus outdoor wear. Recent boom is in the running and outdoor sectors. In particular, young women are taking up these activities, fuelling a desire for brightly coloured and excellently designed products and innovative ones such as so-called "yama-ska" which means mountain skirts. Japanese women are increasingly engaging in sporting activities such as fishing which traditionally were not of interest to them.

The Japanese market often wants customized products, especially in terms of size to fit for the Asian body and colour schemes.

Conclusion

Fact file

- Official name - Japan
- Population - 127, 078, 679
- Official language - Japanese
- Currency - Yen
- Capital city - Tokyo
- GDP - purchasing power parity $4.2348 trillion
- GDP per capita - purchasing power parity $34,300

Japan is the land of peace and harmony that continues to evolve in a positive unification of tradition and modernisation. With its elaborate and colourful history and culture, Japan has formed a distinct model of hierarchy, honour and etiquette that is still reflected in many social and business practices today. If your organisation is planning to conduct business with Japan, potential success depends upon an understanding of this culturally influenced protocol.

Japanese Culture - Key Concepts and Values

Wa - The most valued principle still alive in Japanese society today is the concept of 'wa', or 'harmony'. The preservation of social harmony dates back to the first constitution in 604 AD and the teamwork needed when living and working on collective farms.

In business terms, 'wa' is reflected in the avoidance of self-assertion and individualism and the preservation of good relationships despite differences in opinion. When doing business with the Japanese it is also important to remember the affect of 'wa' on many patterns of Japanese behaviour, in particular their indirect expression of 'no'.

Kao - One of the fundamental factors of the Japanese social system is the notion of 'face'. Face is a mark of personal pride and forms the basis of an individual's reputation and social status. Preservation of face comes through avoiding confrontations and direct criticism wherever possible. In Japan, causing someone to lose face can be disastrous for business relationships.

Omoiyari - Closely linked to the concepts of 'wa' and 'kao', 'omoiyari' relates to the sense of empathy and loyalty encouraged in Japanese society and practiced in Japanese business culture. In literal terms it means "to imagine another's feelings", therefore building a strong relationship based on trust and mutual feeling is vital for business success in Japan.

The late 19th and early 20th centuries saw Japan swiftly embrace the numerous influences of western technology. Following the country's defeat in WWII, Japan experienced a remarkable growth in its economy and fast became the world's most successful exporter. Since then, Japan's business and economy has witnessed a wavering of strengths, however today, Japan is one of the world's leading industrial powers with a new, stable and exciting business market open to foreign investment and trade.

(Do's and Don'ts)

- DO use apologies where the intention is serious and express gratitude frequently as it is considered polite in Japan.
- DO avoid confrontation or showing negative emotions during business negations. Express opinions openly but evade direct or aggressive refusals.
- DO greet your counterparts with the proper respect and politeness. If your counterpart bows make sure you return the gesture, which is usually performed shortly and shallowly. More often than not, a handshake is sufficient.

- DON'T give excessive praise or encouragement to a single Japanese colleague in front of others. Remember that the group is often more important than the individual.
- DON'T address your Japanese counterpart by their first name unless invited to do so. Use the titles 'Mr' or 'Mrs' or add 'san' to their family name; for example, Mr Hiroshima will be "Hiroshima san"
- DON'T use large hand gestures, unusual facial expressions or dramatic movements. The Japanese do not talk with their hands.

Japanese Culture Quiz - True or False
1. In business meetings it is customary for the most senior person to enter the room last and sit closest to the door.
2. In Japanese the number 4 sounds like the word for 'death' and consequently is deemed unlucky.
3. As in many Western cultures, silence is seen as uncomfortable and avoided where possible.
4. In Japanese culture, laughter is often used to hide feelings such as nervousness, shock, embarrassment, confusion and disapproval.
5. It is not rude to slurp or make noise while eating noodles or drinking tea.

Cultural Quiz - Answers
1. False. The most senior member of the team generally enters the room first, followed by his subordinates in order of rank. The least senior member will sit closest to the door.
2. True.
3. False. Silence is often used as part of the thought process and is never thought of as uncomfortable.
4. True. It is generally used when it is not known what feelings to express.
5. True. It is a positive sign that you are enjoying it!

Japan was never a western colony and that is not a coincidence, but largely due to Japanese people's strong will and traditional abilities. (Thailand is another Asian country which was never a western colony.)

Some - but by far not all - western companies find it difficult to succeed in Japan. Reasons include:

- Japanese customers can be very demanding, and often have quit different tastes and needs than Western customers. Therefore in many cases western companies must redesign or redevelop products in order to succeed with Japanese customers. Examples where this is the case range from baby napkins, to tooth brushes, cars and mobile phones.

- Because of Japan's size, substantial investments are necessary, and therefore the inherent risks are also large: you either win big, or lose big.

- Japan has many very strong local companies. As an example, eBay lost in Japan against local competition and withdrew from Japan. Japanese companies also will not usually welcome a new competitor, but develop strategies to compete hard against new entrants. You must be prepared for such competition with very thorough market research and strategy development. If you do not thoroughly understand your competition in Japan, you have little chance to win. In order to win in Japan you must understand and must be prepared and able and willing to compete with local competition.

- Management methods and the actual managers at headquarters in US and EU have certainly won many achievements in the US and Europe and elsewhere. In many cases, however, Western managers and Western management teams are ill prepared to succeed in Japan. In many cases, drastic changes in thinking and management methods and personnel changes at headquarters would be necessary to succeed in Japan. However, there are not many Western companies, which act on this knowledge.

- One critical difficulty, which often is the primary reason for failure in Japan, is simply that not enough or not the right market research is done.

Japan is open for business. This includes Tokyo and surrounding areas, as well as Western Japan which was not directly affected by the earthquake and its aftermath. There are some localised exceptions, primarily around the Fukushima Daiichi Nuclear Power Plant, and coastal areas in north-east Japan. For the latest information you should check FCO travel advice.

It is therefore a good time for UK companies and business to enter or further explore the Japanese market. Japanese companies are looking for assistance in meeting the considerable challenges posed by the disaster and its aftermath.

There are therefore a number of opportunities for UK companies with particular expertise in areas such as: computing, low carbon technologies, energy generation, nuclear decommissioning, business continuity and life sciences/healthcare.

Good Luck!

www.ingramcontent.com/pod-product-compliance
Lightning Source LLC
Chambersburg PA
CBHW051732170526
45167CB00002B/910